GOTCHA! DEADLIEST ANIMALS

DEADLY ANIMALS FOR KIDS
CHILDREN'S SAFETY BOOKS

Speedy Publishing LLC

40 E. Main St. #1156

Newark, DE 19711

www.speedypublishing.com

Copyright 2017

In this book, we're going to talk about some of the deadliest animals in the world. So, let's get right to it!

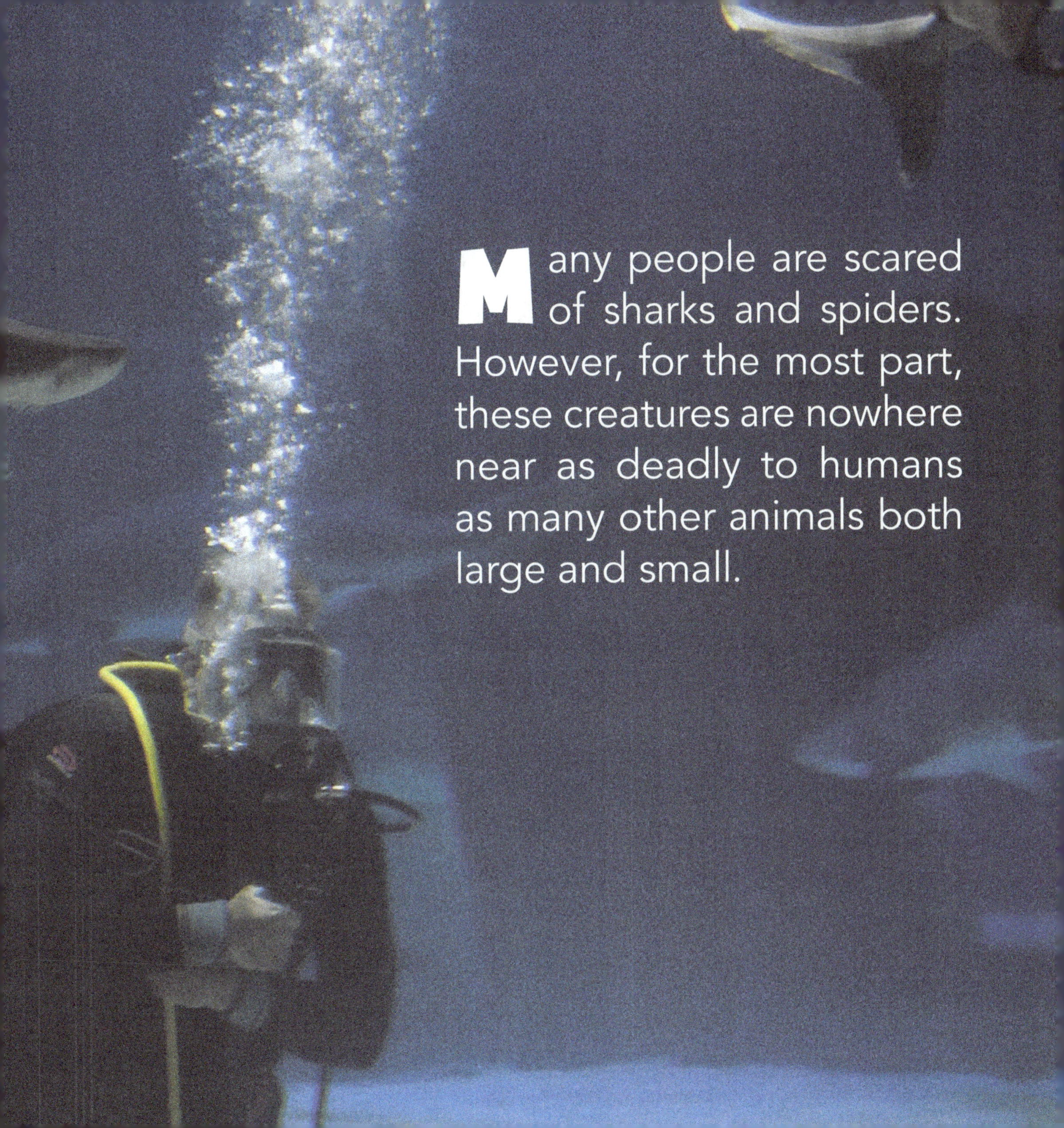

Many people are scared of sharks and spiders. However, for the most part, these creatures are nowhere near as deadly to humans as many other animals both large and small.

CAPE BUFFALO

The Cape buffalo, which lives in the sub-Saharan section of Africa, doesn't really have an aggressive temperament. There are over 900,000 of them and generally they graze on grasses and stay in very large herds for their own protection against predator cats.

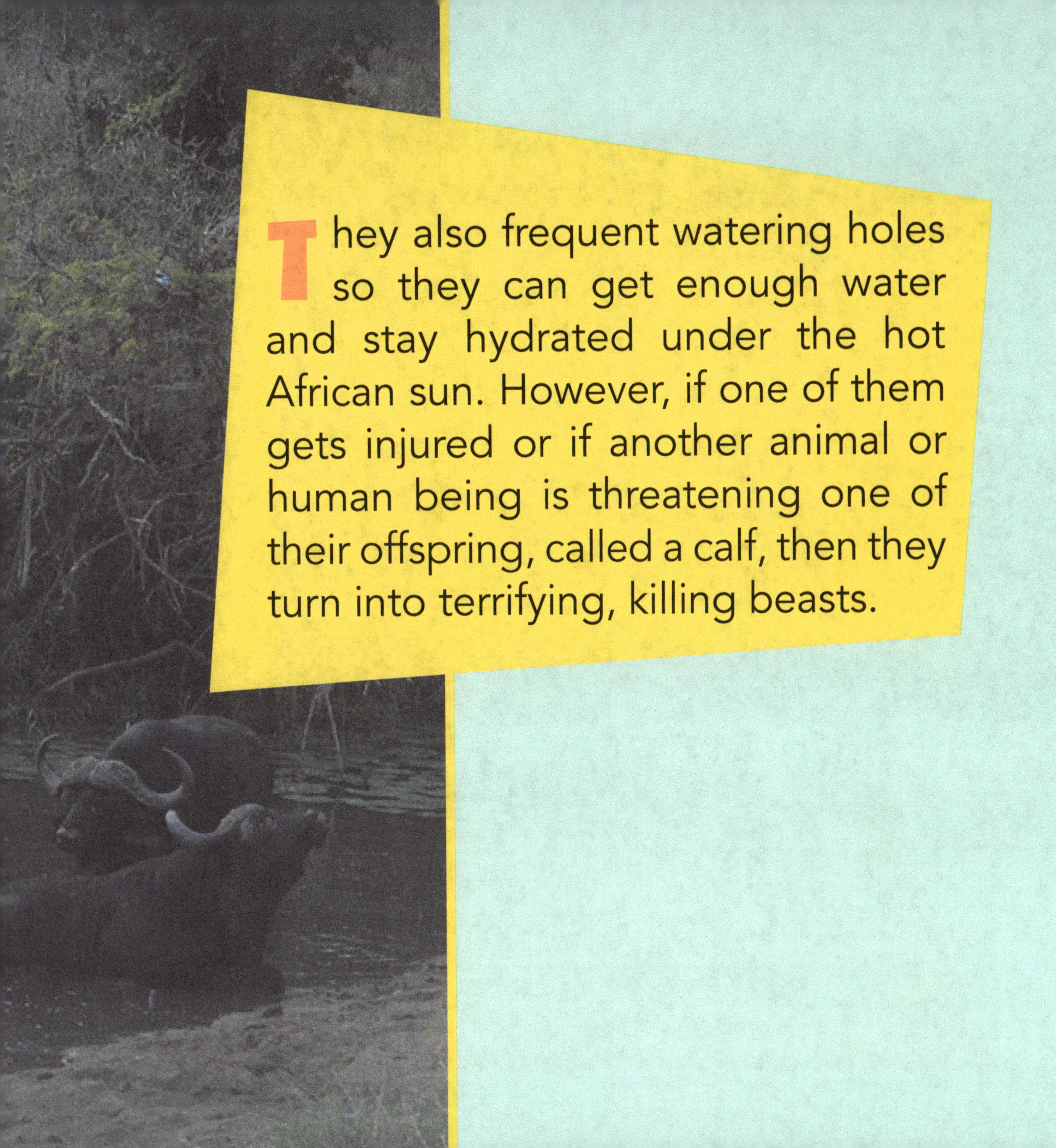

They also frequent watering holes so they can get enough water and stay hydrated under the hot African sun. However, if one of them gets injured or if another animal or human being is threatening one of their offspring, called a calf, then they turn into terrifying, killing beasts.

They can grow to over six feet in height and adult males weigh 1300 pounds or more. They have deadly horns. Before they attack, they circle around their prey whether

it's a person or another animal. Then, they go into a charging attack with their horns forward at speeds of up to 35 miles per hour.

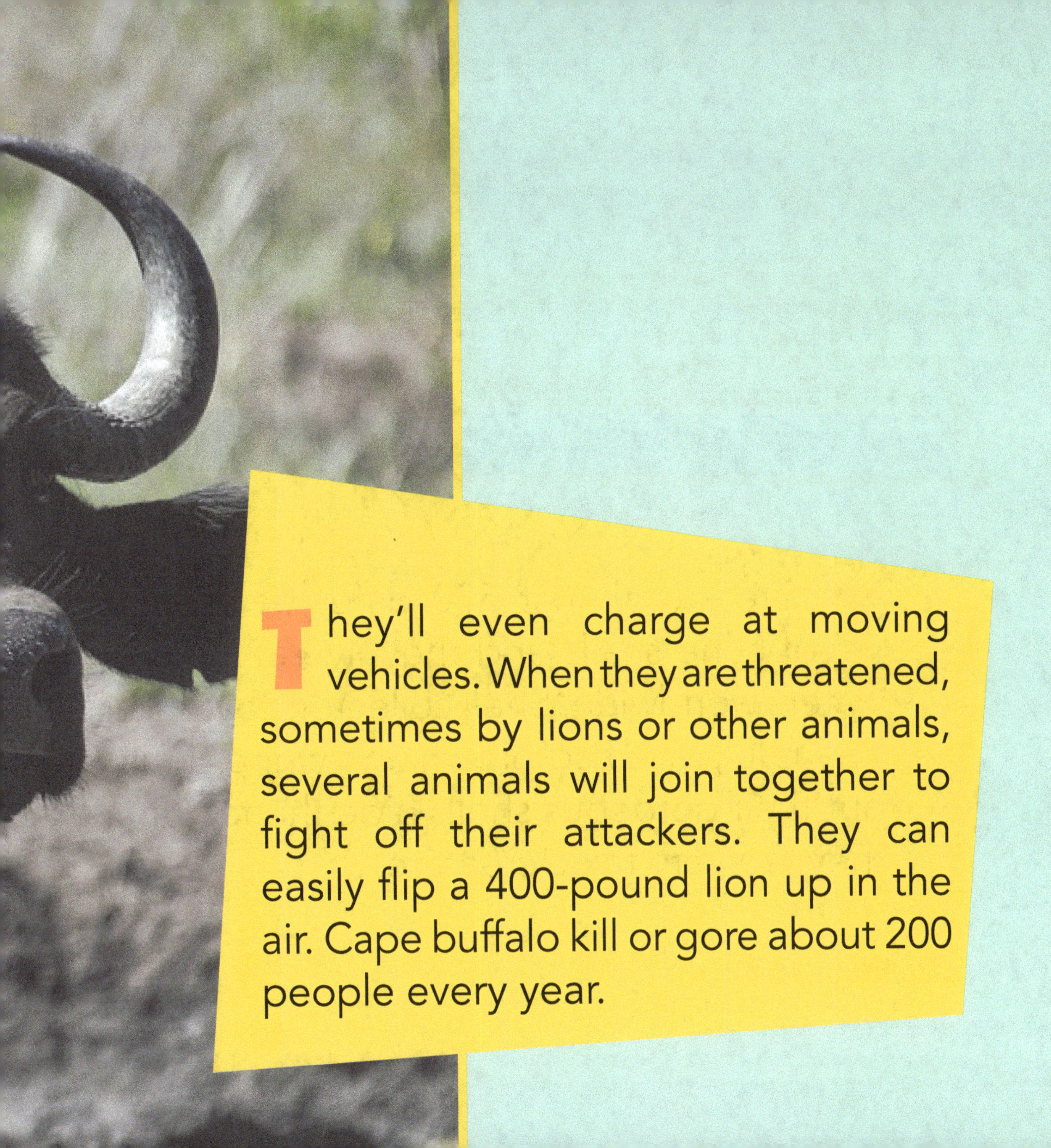

They'll even charge at moving vehicles. When they are threatened, sometimes by lions or other animals, several animals will join together to fight off their attackers. They can easily flip a 400-pound lion up in the air. Cape buffalo kill or gore about 200 people every year.

CONE SNAIL

There are almost 500 different species of cone snails and they live in tropical waters worldwide. Shell collectors love their beautiful, marbled brown and white shells, but their gorgeous shells hide the fact that they are very toxic creatures.

The most dangerous of the cone snails is the 6-inch-long geographic cone, which lives in Indo-Pacific waters. Because it's so slow moving, most gastropods are, it attacks fish with a structure that's like a tooth harpoon. It has a complex venom that is called a conotoxin, which immediately paralyzes the fish so that it can't swim away.

Several people have been killed by this toxin as well since there isn't any antivenom available. Ironically, this same venom has chemical compounds that could be used for pain-fighting drugs.

GOLDEN POISON DART FROG

There are many different types of poison dart frogs. They are native to the northern section of South America. Luckily, only a small number of them are deadly to human beings. The most deadly of them all is the golden poison dart frog. This tiny 2-inch long frog is a beautiful yellow-gold color but its dangerous poison, which is named batrachotoxin, is so toxic that the amount under the frog's skin could potentially kill ten people.

The toxin is so potent that the amount that covers the head of a pin would be enough to quickly kill a human being. The glands where the frog's poison is located are under its skin so touching it is enough to poison you. The native Emberá people figured out a way to get the poison from the frogs to use on their blow darts so that they could kill animals or other natives quickly without hurting themselves.

f you're visiting the rainforests of South America, don't ever touch the small, colorful frogs. The bright colors designate that they are highly poisonous.

BOX JELLYFISH

Hundreds of people die from being stung by box jellyfish every year. These floating invertebrates are almost invisible as they travel through the watery depths. They have box-like transparent bodies and up to 15 tentacles at their corners. Sometimes these tentacles grow to a length of 10 feet. The tentacles have thousands of nematocysts, which are stinging cells that contain dangerous toxins.

A person or animal that is stung by a box jellyfish goes into shock and often succumbs to heart failure before being able to get to shore. There is an antivenom available but even swimmers who survived

and received the antivenom had horrible pain for subsequent weeks and scary scars from the jellyfish's tentacles. Box jellyfish are thought to be the most venomous sea creature worldwide.

PUFFERFISH

Blowfish, also called pufferfish, are brightly colored fish that look harmless enough. However, like other vibrantly colored animals they are highly toxic. They swim in tropical waters worldwide but are found in larger numbers near Japan as well as the Philippines and China.

The only vertebrate that is more poisonous than the pufferfish is the golden poison dart frog. The toxin that pufferfish carry is tetrodoxin and it's located in the skin and muscles of the fish as well as its kidneys, liver, and even its sex organs. In Japan, this fish is considered a gourmet delicacy called fugu.

Because the fish is so poisonous, only chefs who have a special license are allowed to prepare it. In spite of these precautions, several people die each year from eating the fish and receiving the fish's toxin in their meal. Tetradoxin is over 1,000 times more deadly than cyanide. It can cause severe dizziness, vomiting, paralysis of the muscles, and heart irregularities. If the person who ingested the toxin isn't treated, chances are he or she will die. Despite the risks, many people eat pufferfish every year.

BLACK MAMBA

There are many types of poisonous snakes in the world. However, one of the deadliest and perhaps the most dangerous is the black mamba snake. It lives in the savannas as well as the rocky outcroppings in both eastern and southern Africa. This snake is the fastest land snake in the world and can slither along the ground at high speeds of over 12 miles per hour.

It's also a very long snake and grows to a length of up to 14 feet. Luckily, these dangerous snakes only strike when they are threatened. However, if you startled one in the grasses of the savanna, you wouldn't have much chance to survive the event. They strike very quickly and then bite their victims repeatedly.

Their toxins are a deadly combination of neurotoxins and cardiotoxins and one bite could potentially kill 10 people. If you were bitten and didn't have the antivenom injected within 20 minutes, you would die.

SALTWATER CROCODILE

Crocodiles are very dangerous. They have a reputation for being very aggressive towards people or animals that get close even if they are not being threatened. There are many different species of crocodiles worldwide, but by far the most dangerous is the saltwater crocodile called "salties" by the Australians.

They are native to many areas from the coastline of India to Vietnam and in the waters and coastlines south of Vietnam to northern Australia. They are the largest reptile in the world as well as the largest land predator.

Adult males can get up to 23 feet in length and their weight can be more than a ton. They kill hundreds of people every year and are far more deadly than sharks.

If you go swimming in an area where they live, either in freshwater or salt water, you will be attacked with a bite that has a force of the same as one of the deadliest dinosaurs that ever lived on Earth, Tyrannosaurus rex. Humans can only bite at about 5% of the strength of a saltie's bite.

TSETSE FLY

Not all dangerous animals are large. The tsetse fly is a tiny insect that is about the same size as a common housefly. It's found in the countries of Central Africa, such as Angola. The tsetse fly, like a mosquito, bites and then sucks blood during the hottest time of the day.

By themselves, they are harmless enough, but they carry a deadly parasite that is a protozoa called Trypanosomes. These microscopic protozoa cause a disease known as Sleeping Sickness. The sickness attacks the nervous system and causes changes in behavior and coordination as well as changes in sleeping patterns.

Death can be the result if it isn't treated and there are no vaccines that can be used in advance to prevent it. For some reason, the flies are attracted to bright colors as well as dark colors like blue, so wearing light colors and specially-treated clothing helps fend them off.

MOSQUITO

Mosquitoes are even smaller than tsetse flies. There are more than 3,000 different species of mosquitoes and luckily most are not deadly. A few species carry a variety of deadly pathogens, but these are the cause of over 700,000 deaths every year.

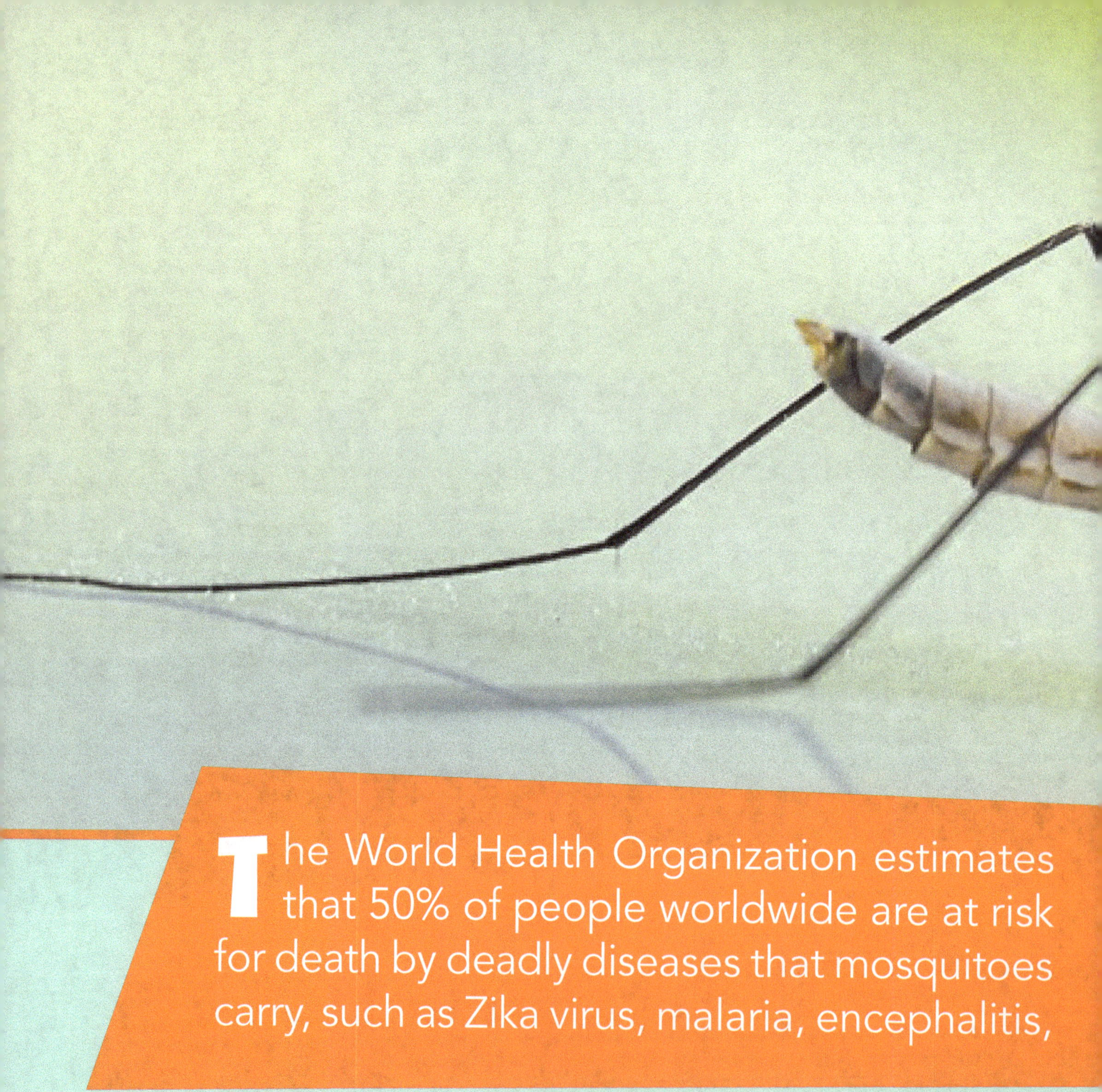
The World Health Organization estimates that 50% of people worldwide are at risk for death by deadly diseases that mosquitoes carry, such as Zika virus, malaria, encephalitis,

and yellow fever. If you're going to an area that has mosquitoes, use insect repellent on your skin to avoid being bitten.

SUMMARY

There are many dangerous animals on land and in the ocean. Some of them are large and have powerful jaws. Others are very tiny but are still dangerous because of the pathogens they carry. When you travel into remote areas, you should make sure you know which types of animals to avoid. Brightly colored amphibians and snakes are often poisonous.

Awesome! Now that you've read about some of the deadliest animals in the world you may want to read about another deadly animal, the Great White Shark, in the Baby Professor book *Swim Away! Swim Away! The Great White Shark Is After Me! Animal Book 4-6 | Children's Animal Books.*

Visit

BABY PROFESSOR
EDUCATION KIDS

www.BabyProfessorBooks.com

to download Free Baby Professor eBooks
and view our catalog of new and exciting
Children's Books

9 798869 416490